Cultivate

Your
Happy Now

Become Beautifully Rooted in Happiness
by Activating These
52 Weekly Power-Packed Motivations

Christy Vance-Tribble

Disclaimer:
The motivational statements you are about to witness serves as a source of valuable insights and consideration for the reader; however, these statements should not serve as direct expert advice or assistance. Readers should seek a competent professional should this type of expertise be required. These statements' two primary goals are to share my perspectives and offer my readers a different approach towards looking inward. I hope you will engage and allow these motivational messages to elevate your Happiness in the moment of NOW!

ACKNOWLEDGMENTS

To my handsome husband, _Tommy Tribble_: Your support and encouragement have carried me through many goals I have set out to achieve. I cannot think of a better person to share these beautiful blessings with. I love how we _Cultivate Our Happiness!_ God has His hands all over our lives, and the best is yet to come.

Thank you for believing in the power of "US!"
I love you, baby, without measure!

To my handsome and intelligent son, _Tymori Tribble_: You are the sparkle in my eyes! Everything I do is referenced back to you in some way. Watching you grow from a baby to a strong, educated man has been such a joy to witness. I am so proud of you and the man you are becoming! Keep going higher. Continue to be steadfast in your quest towards living life to its fullest capacity!
I love you, son, past the sun, moon, and stars!

To my beautiful mother, _Betty V. Faucett_: Thank you for always being my rock! Your consistent love and support help me strive for more and become the best possible version of myself. You are truly my best friend, my shopping companion, and my heartbeat! You have taught me well, and I hope I have made you proud.
I love you, Mom!

To my strong and resourceful dad, _Mack L. Faucett_ (deceased): I watched you live your life fearlessly. Some of your lessons were unconventional, but despite it all, you taught us to be strong, go-getters, and never stop until we are satisfied and successful. I know you are looking down on me, and I hope I have made you proud. My love for you is sent up to heaven always & forever!
I love you, Daddy!

To my beautiful sister, _Kymberly Grant_, and my handsome brother, _Brad Vance_: Thank you for always showing support in all the things I strive to achieve. You both hold an extraordinary special place in my heart. Both of you have your own unique way of expressing your love toward me. A **treasure of a sister and brother's love** is one that stays with you always. Our bond is unbreakable, and I am so glad God blessed me with you. You both are bright spots in my life, and I love you both to pieces!

To my readers: Thank you for supporting me and purchasing my book of weekly motivations. These informative inspirations will help you realize that you should not wait to be happy. Do the opposite! Snatch your happiness now and unlock the many benefits and rewards it has to offer!

DEDICATION

This book is dedicated to the sister, who struggles to elevate her happiness from humdrum to phenomenal. You deserve the opportunity to soar toward vitalizing happiness that is fit for a queen. These motivating words are also dedicated to my brother, who needs a roadmap that leads him out of shackled thoughts and debilitating strongholds. I want you to know that you, too, deserve the opportunity to leap into vitalizing happiness that is fit for a king. Even young adults can pick up this book and get inspired to cultivate happiness. With everything going on around us today, my goal is to help spread **world happiness** to all, one motivating statement at a time, through my new book, *Cultivate Your Happy Now*.

Always begin with **Happiness!**

Sisters ~ Brothers ~ Young Adults

CONTENTS

INTRODUCTION

Many of us put off our happiness to achieve things that do not truly fulfill us. We often tell ourselves, "I will be happy when I get my new home" or, "I will be happy when I get married and have kids." Why wait? Possessing a happy state of mind now sets the stage for gratifying happiness later when you are blessed to receive that new home or marriage. This book offers simple, easy to understand, weekly, motivational statements that will arouse your inner core to cultivate or grow your happiness profusely. Speaking these motivating statements aloud weekly and homing in on their intended purpose will undoubtedly elevate your happiness. Each message in this book begins with bold action words to help grab your attention. Allow these action words to challenge and encourage you to choose to live in happiness now.

My insight into seeking true happiness comes through personal experiences and a few failures along my journey. There have been lots of twists and turns that have slowed me down and caused me to stumble. Let us not mention some of the unexpected detours that showed up and took me off the main road of life. However, by God's Grace and Mercy, I was able to realign and proceed again on a more promising route. I simply activated my faith and gave all my missteps to God. Presently, I vow to be happy in every moment I am blessed to experience. God gets all the Glory! There will be no more putting off my happiness in place of short-lived moments and worldly things that eventually lose its pizzaz! When I rise each day, one of my first choices is to put on a happy mindset to conquer my day ahead.

These weekly motivational statements have also helped other people that are dear to me, such as my sister, Kymberly Grant. Life sometimes gives us lemons, but we must choose to learn how to make fabulous tasting lemonade! I often give my sister advice on many areas of her life. Given that I have been through similar experiences, I motivate her with different viewpoints and touching words that help her shape and mold a happier mindset. She will tell you, "My sister is the most positive and motivating person I know." I love giving people positive wisdom that inspires them to find and highlight happiness in their journeys. If my words can help one or two people cultivate happiness, then my book was well worth the effort and time.

Stop procrastination in its tracks, and do not allow it to be an excuse any longer. Be intentional. Make the promise to yourself to use these 52-weekly, power-packed motivations to soar your happiness to new heights.

"Spiral Symbol"

*Consciousness * Centering * Connection*

*Balance * Journeying*

Throughout this book, the spiral symbol represents inward and outward winding journeys that we must travel to know and love ourselves intimately. These journeys are essential for growth and elevation toward new levels of power and wisdom. However, the journey cannot prosper without the consistent seeking of obtaining a *Happiness Now Mentality!*

Best of luck on your journey!

Your Daily P's

Prayer, Praise, & Perspective

PRAYER & PRAISE

COMMIT to giving consistent prayer and your highest praise to your Creator each day you rise. Give honor to your Creator by acknowledging his:

Royal Presence
Abundant Grace
Infinite Mercy

Adopting this perspective will help *anchor you,* act as your *guiding light,* and *move you graciously* throughout your daily journey.

To commit means to dedicate yourself to something entirely.
Before your feet hit the ground, dedicate yourself to never-ending
prayer and praise towards all the magnificent blessings our Father
has bestowed upon us.

YOUR DAILY PRAYER

COMPOSE your very own motivational prayer below to help your first steps of the day be fueled with power and positivity. Commit to saying this prayer aloud daily.

"Prayer should be the key of the day and the lock of the night."

-George Herbert

_____

_____

_____

_____

_____

_____

_____

_____

PERSPECTIVE

Regarding happiness, write down your perspective of the following image.

Write **Empty** or **Full** in the space provided below.

Answer: _____

Why? _____

_____

_____

_____

"Oneness"

Increase Your Sense of Flow and Personal Fulfillment

In this section, you will explore motivations that can build and generate perpetual happiness within yourself first. Happiness starts with one seed and one root…...YOU!

Let us begin learning how to tap into your "Oneness."

Week 1

ASPIRE always to make a conscious effort to be happy presently, at this very moment, right where you are. Never delay or put off happiness that can be achieved now. Enjoy your *happy* no matter what timeframe you may be placed upon. Live in happiness today because tomorrow is not promised!

Each precious day you are given,
vow to be abundantly happy right where your feet are planted.
Take ownership and make it your lifestyle.

Week 2

MAGNIFY your gratitude. Expressing gratitude is significant in achieving the fullness of a happier you. Count your blessings and be thankful for everything you have – no matter how minuscule or monumental.

*Display thanksgiving at every turn
and every corner to unlock your blessings.*

Week 3

POUR happy thoughts and positive thinking into your mindset. Ward off and distance yourself from all negativity if possible. Negative self-talk is also on the list of things not to do. What you tell yourself matters. We sometimes become the exact thing we think in our minds. Be positive not only in what you speak but in your unspoken words as well. The power of positivity connects so many internal dots that help foster a happy environment within. Regularly practicing this behavior is essential for fueling what feeds the inner you. Good vibes in equate to good vibes out!

You are the gatekeeper of what enters your thoughts.
Guard the entrance well!

Week 4

SPARK up happy beliefs by using "I am" affirmations. This habit builds confidence and faith within plus promotes exceptional strength at your core. Indulge often in this powerful practice and set yourself up for success. Speak your "I am…" affirmations aloud with authority and dominion for best results.

> *I am happy on purpose.*
> *I am happy in my own skin.*
> *I am smart.*
> *I am more than enough.*
> *I am beautiful.*
> *I am amazing.*
> *I am open to receiving goodness and happiness.*
> *I am living my life with gratefulness.*
> *I am much more than the sum of my experiences.*

When you speak positivity over yourself,
it can change outlooks and outcomes.

Week 5

RETREAT to your quiet place often. Seek solitude and stillness from the world, social media, and overall noise in your mind. Allow yourself time to pause. Often, we forget about ourselves due to caring for others and making sure other responsibilities are aligned. Remember, you are important too! Practicing stillness soothes, rejuvenates, and allows you to reset your compass and navigate the world with a clearer mindset.

Break your routine, detach, tune out, and recharge your batteries. Mentally unplugging from your crazy, busy lifestyle is essential for managing your overall well-being.

Week 6

CHOOSE to find the benefit and meaning in your pain. Being happy does not cancel out cloudy and rainy days. Sometimes our lives will face difficulty. In these moments, recognize and learn from what is going wrong. How you choose to respond is the lesson and the key. Learning how to avert from familiar pain and difficulty is a sign of growth and strength. Dwelling on your pain is pointless! Find the silver lining in all your moments, whether rainy or sunny (good days, bad days)!

Wisdom comes in all shapes, sizes, forms, and yes, weather patterns too! Always pack your umbrella of faith to help you withstand the storms of life.

Week 7

PERPETUATE healthy eating choices. Fuel your body with adequate, beneficial nutrients that improve your happy state. Staying consistent in putting healthy things into your body fosters life-long habits that build up a healthier temple. Ingest more fruits, veggies, proteins, and sources of fat that set your body up for success, both inwardly and outwardly.

Wouldn't you like to see the future "you" 10, 20, or even 30 years from now? Consistently practicing good eating habits will add years to your life and add a more improved wholesome lifestyle.

Week 8

MINIMIZE laziness. Remember, the body is made for movement. Exercise, exercise, exercise! Even a burst of laughter is healthy on occasion. Laughter is known to stimulate endorphins (happy hormones) in your brain. This type of facial movement awakens specific facial muscles that you do not usually use. Try tapping into this territory often for feelings of euphoria and general well-being. Being in a prolonged idle state long-term can affect the entire body. Ugly disorders such as osteoporosis, blood clots, confusion, stiffness, and even constipation will rear their ugly heads when the body is not moving regularly.

Studies show that exercising at least 30 minutes can improve your quality of life. Get moving and indulge in a good laugh or two while power walking your way to your happy goals.

Week 9

FOCUS on your strengths rather than your weaknesses. According to some studies, developing our strengths first helps equip us with the promotion of growth, reduced stress, higher confidence, and even elevated happiness. Work on improving where you are **already** strong to cultivate a growth mindset. This behavior plants the seed that you believe in yourself initially and helps lay the foundation. Often weaknesses will fall in line as your strengths are being highlighted.

Having this strength-based mindset will allow your happy journey to take shape more rapidly.

Week 10

PRACTICE POWER POSING.

Standing with a power posture for a few minutes as if you have just won a race can possibly lower the stress hormone, decrease cortisol levels, and elevate testosterone in the brain. This technique can be especially effective just before giving a speech, for example. Power posing may have a considerable impact on your mood and act as a major confidence booster.

Change your posture!
Incorporate this technique into your daily routine for maximized confidence and feelings of increased power.

Week 11

COLOR your Mondays with a hefty dose of *Happy*. Mondays usually have a negative stigma of being a low energy day. Do not feed into this hype. Erase this negative perception and allow your day to be bright and vibrant no matter what day it is!

When life gives you Monday, always color it Happy.

Week 12

REMOVE negative scenarios from your mindset. Never imagine failure, embarrassment, fear, or the worst of everything. Build yourself up to visualize detailed images of your winning and succeeding. Promoting positive images of yourself in your mind builds tremendous confidence. How you see yourself makes all the difference in the world. Remember, there is power in your thoughts!

Give yourself constant reminders that you can win in any situation no matter what! Negativity is never an option.

Week 13

EMBRACE your challenges.

"Happiness lies in the joy of achievement and
the thrill of creative effort."

-Franklin D. Roosevelt

*Force yourself to look beyond your difficulties and seek solutions.
You may even find yourself rising to greater heights and
experiences.*

Difficulties can also be beautiful teachings!

21

REFLECTIONS

CONSIDER what takeaways from **section one** you can apply to your life to *Cultivate Your Happiness Now.*

Which motivation stood out to you the most? Why?

_____

_____

_____

_____

_____

_____

_____

_____

Display Happiness to Others

This next section speaks upon ways to elevate your awareness and happiness meter towards people.

Previously, I mentioned how to build happiness within yourself, first, through oneness. Now devote your attention to these next several pages on spreading and showcasing your happiness to others.

Week 14

PAY IT FORWARD.

Share an act of kindness with a stranger or someone you know personally. A simple, kind word or a small monetary gesture may go a long way in helping to brighten up someone's day. As you elevate your happiness, be a blessing to someone less fortunate. Remember, it is not always about you. Share your knowledge, your gifts, and your good fortune with others.

If you don't succeed at anything else in life,
learn how to be kind to others – look around, look back, be an
unexpected blessing to someone this week.

Make it an ongoing habit!

Week 15

LEAN on systems that help support and elevate you forward. Having a sound support system, whether it is family, a good friend to lean on, or something you can identify with to bring out positivity, can be a huge lifesaver! Build up your network of protection and use it when you need that necessary boost.

Simply go sit down with a friend or your support system and get energized. Sometimes this is all the medicine you need to help navigate your happiness today, tomorrow, and beyond.

Week 16

THROW out the judgment of others and the judgment of yourself. There is no gain in pre-assumptions because it is wasteful and unproductive energy. Possessing a judging spirit is exhausting and adds an unnecessary layer of ugliness to your appearance.

Try never to judge.

Keep your inner self free from these nasty tendencies.
Do not allow these energy robbers to take
control of your peaceful territory within.

Week 17

SHOWCASE your beautiful happiness to others. Make it a point always to aim to be pleasant when people occupy your space. Ensure everyone you meet leaves your company a little happier than they arrived. Practice giving out good vibrations. Happiness is very contagious, so be sure you spread it well.

Stay armed with a happy persona.

Week 18

GUARD your happiness at all entrances. People will try to steal your joy intentionally and unintentionally. Be aware of these thieves and avoid them at all costs! You are the gatekeeper of your happiness. Carefully screen whom you allow on your journey and recognize when to eject people off your journey!

Put up a "<u>No Trespassing</u>" sign and surround yourself with like-minded people who always support your happy journey.

Week 19

EXAMINE your surroundings. Everything is not always a nuisance. This week give your attention to something or someone you would otherwise disregard. Consider holding a conversation with the slow bag boy in the grocery line instead of frowning, or simply offer to buy a homeless person a meal for the day. Become increasingly aware of your surroundings.

Do not discount people and allow yourself to become annoyed quickly. Look up often and realize happiness can also be found in your everyday, ordinary surroundings.

Give your attention to others happily.

Week 20

DEVELOP a spirit of forgiveness. Free yourself from holding on to heaviness. Allow yourself to let go of grudges towards others, resentments, and darkness. Releasing these things will unlock more room for abundance within. Do not block your blessings by having an unforgiving heart.

Forgive quickly.

Forgive yourself as well!
Your heart needs room to receive other Godly things that are much
more important than harboring unforgiveness.

Week 21

TRAIN yourself never to compartmentalize your happiness. Allowing yourself to be happy around certain people just to fit in or casting your happiness to the side only to accommodate certain situations is senseless and quite exhausting. One's happiness should never be turned on and off like a switch. Be proud of your happy journey, no matter what or who is around. Always keep your happiness in a rhythm of harmony.

Be you!
Be happy!
No excuses!

Week 22

DON'T LAYER unhealthy things such as:

Heaviness	Toxic People	Negativity
Doubt	Over-Eating	Blame
Greed	Wastefulness	Grudges
Jealousy	Bitterness	Envy
Guilt	Unhappiness	Hatred

Feelings of Lack

Unforgiveness

Mean Spirit

Racism

Apply positive layers to your day that helps elevate and motivate you towards pure happiness.

Week 23

"**BE** the living expression of God's kindness; kindness in your face, kindness in your eyes, kindness in your smile."

-Mother Teresa

Your face is your personal signature. It is a representation of who you are. Face the world with your signature look by expressing a face full of kindness. Now, imagine everyone wearing a face full of kindness. What a magnificent world portruit this would be!

Do your part!

Week 24

TIE your happiness to ambition rather than people. We usually lose sight of our happiness through short-lived tangibles -- things we think will make us happy. Let us be clear, people will let us down, and things will not hold our happiness long term.

Setting our sights on reachable goals and minimizing the need to please people and obtain things will certainly create fulfillment and a more peaceful heart.

Week 25

ANNOUNCE your happiness to the world!

"Hello Happiness"

Start your day with intentional happiness. You cannot go wrong when choosing to start your day with a happy, upbeat mindset. When your happiness is genuine, others can clearly see it and benefit.

Speak it, embrace it, declare it, and confront everything with a hefty dose of Happy each beautiful day!

Week 26

RECOGNIZE that having fun is temporary but a necessary step on the happiness journey. Find ways to combine fun and meaningfulness. Take note that fun without meaning is only temporary and meaning without fun is merely humdrum. Some would call it plain boring! The two should always work together so you can have a more lasting, memorable experience!

Have some awesome fun, but
also, remember to seek meaning for your moments.
Connecting these two critical points will allow your experiences to
manifest into great memories for yourself and others.

REFLECTIONS

SPEAK a motivation into existence from **section two** for your life currently. Actions most certainly speak louder than words.

Start now and change the way you do your *Happiness*!

_____

_____

_____

_____

_____

_____

_____

_____

"Wealth"

Happiness Beyond the Money

This powerful section brings light towards how you approach your money and how to build wealth within that is far better than any dollar amount.

Focus on how to achieve great wealth inside your hands as well as outside of your hands.

Week 27

UNDERSTAND that money has a greater meaning and worth connected to it. Wealth equates to having resources to pull from, such as family, good friends, health, and an abundance of joy. The money will not always complete you, but recognizing and tapping into the extraordinary value of life's other precious treasures will without, a doubt, help balance things out.

Money is not everything but marrying it with more of life's non-monetary treasures makes you exceedingly rich!

Week 28

TAKE INVENTORY! "It's good to have money and the things that money can buy, but it's good, too, to check up once in a while and make sure that you haven't lost the things that money can't buy."

– George Lorimer

As you increase your wealth,
give much attention to your overall happiness, such as peace
within, self-love, family happiness, and love for others.
Precious qualities such as these cannot be bought with money.
Nurture these rarities and strive to house all these gems in one
package deal.

Separately, these gems lose their light.
Together, they illuminate the sky!

Week 29

SUSTAIN your sweet spot on the fulfillment curve as it relates to money. Be careful toggling between comfort and luxury. Overcompensating in the luxury zone can tend to get out of control, especially when it starts to detract from your fulfillment of having enough. For example, an average cup of coffee from your local coffee shop should be enough to satisfy you. Things tend to spiral out of control when you think that mail ordering the Kona coffee bean from Hawaii each month is sound judgment. Fulfilling your coffee craving should not come with a lavish price tag. This type of behavior, whether it is coffee or something else, leads to overspending. It also gives the illusion that you are happy because you possess luxurious things, brands, or more money.

Always staying aware of that inner voice that whispers, "more is always better," will help you balance your overcompensating tendencies, whether it is money or otherwise.

Week 30

ALIGN your money with intentional meaning and clearly defined goals. Constant frivolous spending or senseless spending leads to a disastrous road ahead. Form money habits that help elevate you. Consciously become aware of how you receive money in your hands and how money leaves out of your hands. Just because you have an extra $500 set aside does not mean you need to go splurge extravagantly. Good financial behavior is critical in dealing with credit, owning a home, obtaining good interest rates, and confidently possessing that great feeling of freedom in your finances.

Educating yourself with good money knowledge is a powerful tool. Merging this money knowledge with happiness will enable you to climb the wealth ladder better prepared, joyful, and optimistically prosperous.

Week 31

DEPOSIT unfaltering faith in the universal bank that God has set upon us. Familiarize yourself with how the power of faith can move the needle or produce miraculous wonders in your life. When you go to God with a thimble level of trust, do not be surprised if He answers you with a thimble level of blessings. Often, we have not because we ask not. **God's Glory** is unlimited, and his kingdom is grand! Eloquently as it was, the sun, moon, stars, and earth itself was created by God.

Withdraw from the universal bank with your prayers.
Be amazed at how God will often bless you
just by <u>Simply Asking</u> befittingly!

Week 32

LIVE RICHLY in the Creator's will that you have the abundance of His kingdom at your fingertips. God wants you to be rich in every way possible because you have been born into royalty. You are created in an image of His likeness with incredible and powerful knowledge within. He does not want you to ever live in lack or need. The inheritance your Father has given you is more than enough. The wealth of the world and the universe is rightfully yours to possess.

Thank you, Father, for all I have been given.
I claim and accept all my riches.

In return, I praise your holy name daily!

Week 33

IGNORE money when the tendency of greed surfaces. If you are always thinking of money, how to get it, chasing it, coming up with quick attempts to gain it, and allowing money to invade and take over your mind, you will always have a lack of it or go without it. The money source works better when you do what you do without the great expectation of money. Channels open when the stigma of "hustled money" is removed. The unexpected happens when you remove the fixation and focus on money. Often, money will just land right into your hands when the spotlight is zoomed in on the purpose and not the amount.

Real purpose always wins over the reward of money as it relates to peace within. If money is for you, it will be available to you without any forced efforts.

Week 34

TOSS aside the old mentality and insights on money matters that your parents once had. Under no circumstances should you ever be afraid to talk about money. I remember growing up watching my dad handle all the household finances. Looking back on things today, I do not agree with some of his money tactics. Always ask questions and gain knowledge on how to grow and understand your money. Inform your children at young ages how to handle money responsibly, now rather than later. In today's changing world, money certainly makes things happen. We all must prepare and equip ourselves with the best money knowledge to stay ahead in such a money-driven society.

Invest in yourself and start growing your wealth knowledge towards a more sustained future.

Week 35

VALUE your time over money always. You can earn more money, but you cannot replace time. While we are heavily invested in the sprint to pursue our money goals, we lose sight of the one thing you can never get back, which is our precious time. We must seize the precious moments more and force ourselves to acknowledge that time is consistent and unstoppable. Before you know it, months and years go by unnoticed. Choose to soak in your surroundings rather than allowing money to be dominant over your life.

Money has its place in the world, but time is precious and waits for no one. Allocate your time well.

Week 36

PILE up your riches by the service you do in the world. Your reputation can make you very wealthy. In all that you do, try your best to do it well. Be a person of your word, set a positive example, and always put your best foot forward. Groom your children to continue your excellent work, teach them to be dependable, reliable, and honest. Always make a memorable impression when service is required of you. Your work and how it represents you is your greatest attribute.

Be rich in the service you give to others. Money is not always your greatest asset; your service also holds significant value.

Serve well!

Week 37

OBSERVE the flow of the universe. Movement and order are essential to what you possess in life. If your affairs are not in order, you cannot expect a positive flow of abundance. If you owe someone, you must pay them what they are due. If you cannot pay, it is your duty to make a consistent agreement to pay something. When things are out of order in our lives, the flow will move right past us without stopping. Divine order is a pathway towards obtaining ultimate prosperity.

To tap into the universal flow, you must strive to live in a certain order to achieve greater in your life.

Stay open and follow the flow closely.

Week 38

DWELL in wealth possibilities. There are so many things around us that have the potential to increase our wealth value. Of course, seeking out the obvious money-makers are a given. Things like obtaining higher-paying positions, winning the lottery, or owning successful businesses, are all candidates for the quest for money. However, tapping into those things that we often overlook or disregard due to its insignificance can also be rewarding. Passion projects, dreams with no wings, unique services that help people, and advocacy work are to name a few. They tend to add a layer of satisfaction that speaks to our souls more.

The wealth wheel has many flavors connected to it.
Don't always get stuck on the green flavor (money).

Week 39

PARTNER with other wealth-minded individuals that will propel you higher. You cannot grow a wealthy mindset with the wrong people around you. There is nothing more stifling than to consistently be surrounded by people who do not share your wealth vision. The key is to learn and grow through guidance, wisdom, examples, body language, and practice. Shifting your thinking to obtain a wealth mindset is extremely hard but necessary if you genuinely seek to increase wealth.

Finding the right family or outlet to help elevate your wealth mindset can lead to your success or failure.

Choose wisely.

REFLECTIONS

HIGHLIGHT the most thought-provoking motivation in **section three**. Are you ready to bring this motivation to life by applying it now to your daily, weekly routine?

"If you want to be happy — Practice!"

-Frank Crane

_____

_____

_____

_____

_____

_____

"Abundance"

Now I Have an Ample Amount of Happiness

You have won the race when you figure out how to achieve an abundance of happiness.

Previously, you learned that you should first be happy within yourself through practicing oneness. Secondly, you learned how to give an outpouring of happiness to others. Thirdly, you were given ideas on how to view wealth in a new light other than monetary. Finally, we close with how to seek and grow happiness abundantly without pause.

Week 40

PAY ATTENTION

"The foolish man seeks happiness in the distance;

the wise grows it under his feet."

– James Oppenheim

Real happiness starts right where you are standing.
Water, fertilize, and nurture its growth to success at the very
beginning (genesis).

Week 41

DO MORE of what is good for your soul. Often, we chase rainbows with no pot of gold at the end of it. This behavior leads to unfulfillment and unhappiness. Start seeking and doing things that awaken your soul. Feel exhilarated when you do the things you love, such as traveling, meditation, running, painting, and spending time with family. Doing more of what you love is one of the many pathways to happiness.

*Whatever your passion is, maximize it
by doing more of it!*

Week 42

PURPOSELY LEARN something new this week. Healthy aging is derived from lifelong learning and staying engaged socially. Learn an enjoyable and stimulating activity or try your hand at something more complex, like learning Spanish or trading stocks.

Happiness and well-being will blossom when new things are continually being learned. Stay stimulated, no matter how old you are.

Remember, you can teach an old dog new tricks!

Week 43

REDUCE your fixation on possessions. Excessive attachment to things is not healthy. Possessions should not define your happiness because they will often come and go. Instead, place your energy on intangible things such as lasting joys, goodwill, simplicity, self-love, love for one another, and Kodak moments. Your possessions are not the underlying problem; it is the excessive value we sometimes place on them that is harmful.

Place your grip towards a joyful heart of peace, and let possessions be what they are without the extra baggage attached.

Week 44

BE INFORMED. The secret sauce to life is choosing to be happy ahead of all things. This type of mindset helps put you on the path to achieve greatness and become your best self. Happiness is more than just a yellow smiley face; it is indeed the path to inner balance and fulfillment. The impact reaches so many essential areas of our life, such as success, goals, relationships, health, and learning.

Once you find that secret sauce to life — which is vowing to armor yourself with a happy core, anything is possible!

Week 45

INCREASE the idea of being happy. Having simple thoughts of increasing your happiness level will start to cultivate happy vibes. Almost everything begins with a simple idea. You owe it to yourself to plant the seed of growing and developing your happiness.

Never underestimate the "seed." Imagine having one thought to take root and multiply your happiness within.

One seed can grow an entire garden of happiness!

 Cultivate Your Happy

Week 46

PRACTICE happy emotions every day:

Upbeat	Cheerful
Optimistic	Joyful
Pleasant	Proudful
Serene	Hopeful
Gracious	Euphoric
Satisfied	Enthusiasm
Inspired	Jovial
Amused	Delightful
Jubilant	Playful
Creative	Blessed
Uplifted	Balanced
Centered	Unhurried

Be unapologetically Happy daily!

Week 47

ACTIVATE healthy eagerness. Most things in life need a bolt of enthusiasm to get them off the ground. Learn how to be your own cheerleader! You are the ruler over how you approach your happiness. Showing excitement is a great first step! Happiness is connected to energy, vitality, creativity, and passion. Get excited now about your happy journey and watch the great reveal come to light.

Many possibilities are connected to your happy journey--
enthusiasm and positive energy rank extremely high
at the top of the list.

Week 48

DREAM while continuing to be actively happy now! As it relates to your personal life, friendships, and career, ponder how you want your life story to unfold. Keep that same *Happiness Now Mentality* that we have been talking about in this book. Remember, you are in the process of cultivating your happiness in the moment of **NOW!**

*Your happy mindset is already rock solid.
New blessings will just sweeten the playing
field.*

Happily, receive your beautiful blessings.

Week 48 (continued)

This week spend five minutes each day capturing your thoughts and dreams while exercising your *Happiness Now Mentality.*

Example 1:
A new home will only add to my already happy and fulfilled life!

Example 2:
The happiness I feel right now will compliment how I will feel when I get my master's degree.

_____

_____

_____

_____

_____

_____

Week 49

REFLECT upon what you have now. Be thankful for the blessings you have been given thus far. If you cannot be happy with your current blessings, you will always seek people, places, and things to later validate your happiness.

If you love what you are blessed with right now, you will absolutely adore what God has in store for you on the journey to happiness ahead!

God bless my everything!

Week 50

KEEP GOING and realize that your road ahead will sometimes have twists, turns, detours, warnings, and even forks in the road. The happy journey is not always a straight, perfect road. Persistence is key! Choosing to be happy is a choice, but it comes with hard work and constant practice. Things will appear in your path to test you but stay the course.

*Many roads lead to
the happiness destination – some are short routes;
some much longer, but always remember to keep going.*

Week 51

Trust

Believe

Divine Power

Open your Mind

Miracles, Signs, & Wonders!

May God's footsteps enter your private door (mind and heart),
followed by the many amazing promises of his kingdom.

Week 52

COOK UP your happiness one ingredient at a time. Sprinkle lots of love, pour in patience, stir in good humor, add lots of smiles, fold in positivity, and lastly, shake a packet of life-loving in your everyday journey of happiness.

Life is too short to be anything but happy!
Utilize this happy recipe and make your life amazing!

Fulfillment is guaranteed!

REFLECTIONS

PREPARE your top five motivations to start exercising immediately after reading this book. There is no time like the present to begin manifesting these power-driven motivations into existence. Cultivating your happiness takes consistent commitment. The more you practice, the more you will be prepared for the journey ahead.

"The Beginning is Always Today."

-Mary Wollstonecraft

_____

_____

_____

_____

_____

_____

_____

IMPORTANT ANNOUNCEMENT

Psychology research and the negativity bias inform us that negative to positive thoughts are scaled around a 1:5 ratio to maintain balance. _Simply put, this means you will need five positive thoughts to cancel out or reverse one negative thought._ *Alarming, right?*

Remember, negative thoughts wreak havoc and take root quickly, causing all sorts of unrest inwardly and outwardly. Staying armed with a positive mindset can ward off these invaders from establishing territory and control.

May happiness always light your pathway ahead!
Make a great effort to always keep negativity from entering
your happiness journey.

PERSPECTIVE

Regarding happiness, what is your reaction to the following image now that you have read the book?

Write Empty or Full below.

Answer: _____

Why? _____

_____

_____

_____

_____

FINAL THOUGHT

MEASURE your glass wisely. Understand that having a positive perception always gives you the winning edge. Accepting that your glass is half full gives you hope that you are almost at the top. Accepting that your glass is half empty can also provide hope. The option remains for you to dig deeper and find that strength that keeps you motivated to keep pushing forward. The more you try, the more your glass can reach its fullest potential. It all comes down to the viewing lens you choose to look through. When you approach your glass with just an ounce of positivity, you are giving *power* to helping fill your glass, whether it is half empty or half full.

Happiness and Fullness to You Always!

Other
Acknowledgments

Father, God

Creator of All Things

You get the Glory
You get the Praise
You get the Honor
Halleluiah to Your Name

Thank you for covering me and blessing me
on this beautiful "Book Journey!"

To My Mother-in-law

Nancy

*Thank you for welcoming me into your family
and sharing your heart with me.*

*May happiness be upon you and overflow
throughout your heart, endlessly.*

Grace ~ Strength ~ Mercy

To My Nephew, Nieces, & Stepdaughter:

Khari (KJ)

Belarose (Bela)

Bradesia (Bubbles),

Keyonie (KeKe),

& Shanautica (Nauti)

Bless all that you are becoming, and may happiness take root in your hearts and grow profusely throughout your life always!

Dream ~ Aspire ~ Believe

To My Sister Circle:

Dreicka

Andrea

Shirley

& Pam

May our bond always be held together with love, laughter, experiences, and solidarity! Continuously seek happiness and allow it to infuse within the beautiful layers of your life today, tomorrow & beyond!

Abundance ~ Light ~ Increase

To My Extended Family

Debra

Audrey

Jarod

Michael

Aisha (Ziah & Nola)

Geoffrey

All of you are beautifully rooted in Daddy's "Love."
Miles may separate us, but his "Love"
lives on and keeps us connected.

May you always live in a harmony of happiness!

Elevate ~ Anchor ~ Thrive

Special Thank You

Tammy Carpenter
Effectual Concepts LLC
(Book Formatting Services)

Emme Smith
Minding Your Business Professional
Consulting Services, LLC
(Editor)

Tina Fulton
Unveiled Creations, LLC
(Book Cover Design)

What an amazing journey of connections, learnings, and triumphs we have traveled with the birth of this new book. I will treasure it all and be forever grateful to such a beautiful trio of encouraging, inspiring women.

Thankful ~ Grateful ~ Blessed

ABOUT THE AUTHOR

Christy Vance-Tribble

ABOUT THE AUTHOR

Christy Vance-Tribble is a motivator, encourager, positive thinker, and lover of positive quotes that promote personal elevation. In her first book, _Cultivate Your Happy Now,_ she bravely takes a leap of faith to gift the world inspiring uplifting messages about taking your happiness to higher heights. Christy has always been deeply passionate when it comes to passing on encouragement to others. She offers herself as an accountability partner when needed and expresses unique ways of looking at life through a _happy lens_ rather than a negative viewpoint. Her goal is to reach and teach as many as she can to take ownership of your happiness now so you can become the best version of yourself right where you are – no procrastination allowed!

Christy is a proud graduate of Piedmont Technical College and a long-time employee of the corporate world. For the past 27 years, her entire career path has been with Milliken & Company, located in Spartanburg, SC. She just recently got promoted to the HR platform as an Organizational Management Administrator within the Compensation Team. Before HR, her work background was in Corporate Accounting as a Payment Specialist/Team Leader. In her spare time, Christy loves to appeal to her creative side. Her passion truly lies in making something out of nothing and remixing things to give them that pizazz effect! She dabbles in home décor makeovers, occasionally creates hand-made jewelry, and brings her ideas/visions to life through exercising her unique creativity. Putting trendy clothing combinations together is another pastime she enjoys.

Christy, her husband (Tommy Tribble), and her son (Tymori Tribble) all happily reside in South Carolina.

LET'S STAY CONNECTED

Once you have completed the book, stay connected with me through one of the following outlets:

Amazon:

Purchase a book or two for a colleague, friend, or neighbor. Remember to leave a book review.

Website:

Elevate * Align * Triumph
eatyourway2happiness.com

Email:

elevate.align.triumph@gmail.com

Be Happy, *Be Whole,* ***Be Blessed***

CLOSURE QUOTE

"The beautiful purpose of life is

to live in a capacity of wholeness, and

to live in a capacity of wholeness

simply means

to be *truly enlightened……*

happily, blessedly, serenely, & divinely."

-Christy Vance-Tribble

I AM...

HAPPY NOW

Made in the USA
Columbia, SC
05 January 2021